D1101429

Aberdeenshire Library and Information Service
www.aberdeenshire.gov.uk/libraries
Renewals Hotline 01224 661511

1 6 MAY 2007

2 7 JUN 2008

1 4 APR 2009
2 1 DEC 2012

ABERDEENSHIRE
LIBRARIES

WITHDRAWN
FROM LIBRARY

LLEWELLYN, Claire

Sound and
hearing

A L I S

2561342

START-UP
SCIENCE

SOUND AND HEARING

Claire Llewellyn

Evans

Published by Evans Brothers Limited
2A Portman Mansions
Chiltern Street
London W1U 6NR

© Evans Brothers Limited 2004
Reprinted 2005
Produced for Evans Brothers Limited by
White-Thomson Publishing Ltd.
2/3 St Andrew's Place
Lewes, East Sussex BN7 1UP

Printed in China by WKT Company Limited

Editor: Dereen Taylor
Consultants: Les Jones, Science Consultant, Manchester
Education Partnership, Norah Granger, former primary
headteacher and senior lecturer in education, University
of Brighton
Designer: Leishman Design
Artwork: Peter Wilks

Cover: All photographs by Chris Fairclough.

The right of Claire Llewellyn to be identified as the
author of this work has been asserted by her in
accordance with the Copyright, Designs and Patents
Act 1988.

All rights reserved. No part of this publication may be
reproduced, stored in a retrieval system or transmitted in
any form, or by any means, electronic, mechanical,
photocopying, recording or otherwise, without the prior
permission of Evans Brothers Limited.

British Library Cataloguing in Publication Data
Llewellyn, Claire
   Sound and hearing - (Start-up science)
   1.Sound - Juvenile literature 2. Hearing - Juvenile
   literature
   I.Title
   534

ISBN: 0 237 52645 X

Acknowledgements:
The publishers would like to thank staff and pupils at
Elm Grove Primary School, Brighton, for their
involvement in the preparation of this book.

Picture Acknowledgements:
Chris Fairclough Colour Library 6 (bottom left);
8 (left and right); 9 (left); Corbis 6 (top left, bottom right);
13 (bottom); 16 (main); 17 (right); Ecoscene 4 (right);
7 (bottom left); 18, 19; Eye Ubiquitous 9 (right).
All other photographs by Chris Fairclough.

ABERDEENSHIRE LIBRARY AND	
INFORMATION SERVICES	
2561342	
HJ	494216
J534	£10.99
JU	ROSP

Contents

A sound walk

◄ Dad and Luca are walking to school. They hear a lot of sounds on the way.

► They hear birds singing in the trees.

◄ They hear a motorbike roaring down the street.

hear sounds singing

▲ They hear children shouting in the playground.

What do you hear on your way to school?

roaring shouting

All sorts of sounds

There are many different kinds of sound in the world.

◄ Some are loud, like the engines of a plane.

▲ Some are soft, like the wind in the leaves.

▲ Some are high, like a violin.

▲ Some are low, like a cello.

different   loud   soft   high   low

Look at the things in the pictures on this page. What kinds of sound do they make?

WARNING!
Very loud noises can hurt our ears.

noises   hurt

Different places, different sounds

Different places have their own special sounds.
What would you expect to hear in these places?

Railway station

Wood

How do these sounds make you feel?
What would these places sound like at night?
What different sounds might you hear?

Building site

Beach

feel night

Our bodies make sounds

Our bodies make many different sounds.

We make sounds when we speak and sing.

We can make plenty of other sounds, too!

▼Can you make these sounds?

Whistle!

Clap!

Atchoo!

speak sing breathing quiet

Our bodies make sounds as they work. Can you hear yourself breathing?

▼ Some body sounds are very quiet. You need a stethoscope to hear someone's heart beating.

Pop!

stethoscope   beating

We hear with our ears

▶ We hear sounds with our ears. **Hearing** is one of our body's **senses**.

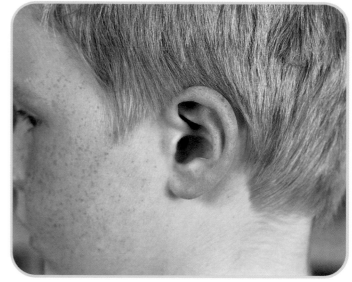

◀ Try closing your eyes and **listening**. What can you hear right now? What do the sounds – or the **silence** – tell you?

hearing   senses   listening   silence

Some people hear better than others.

► Cupping a hand around your ear helps you to hear more clearly.

People who are deaf cannot hear well. They may use a hearing aid and learn to read sign language.

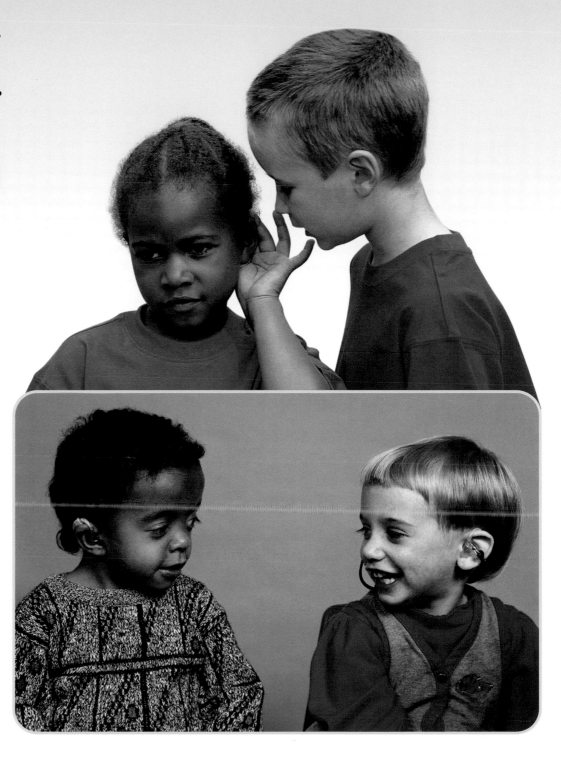

deaf   hearing aid   sign language   13

Near or far?

Our ears tell us where a sound is coming from. They tell us whether the sound is near or far away. Things sound louder the nearer they are.

Kip gives Sam a hearing test. Kip takes one stride back and whispers something softly. Then he moves back two more strides and does it again.

Each time, Sam tells him whether he can hear him or not.

Kip does the same with a whistle.

near far away louder hearing test

Then Lily does the test with some bells.

The chart shows what Sam can hear.

Strides	1	5	10
Whisper	✓	✗	✗
Bells	✓	✓	✗
Whistle	✓	✓	✓

Which sound can Sam only hear close-up?

Which sound can he hear from furthest away?

whispers   whistle   bells

15

Hearing keeps us safe

▲ Our hearing helps to keep us safe. We hear the 'beep beep' sound at the pedestrian crossing. This tells us when it's safe to cross the road.

safe beep beep pedestrian crossing

▼ Drivers may hear a fire engine before they see it. Its siren tells them to clear the road so that it can get to the fire quickly.

▲ Animals also warn us with sound. A guard dog barks and growls to keep people away.

How does a cat show it is angry?

siren warn barks growls

Sound words

There are many different words to describe sounds. These are some of the words we use to describe fireworks:

fizz

sizzle

bang

whizz

whoosh

words   describe

Look at the sound words on this page.
Which ones best describe the sea in this picture?
Can you think of any others?

boom   clap   roar   rattle

tinkle   splash   whine   crash

Which of these pictures do you like best?
Maybe you could write a poem about it.

poem

Sound stories

▲ **These pictures tell a story.**

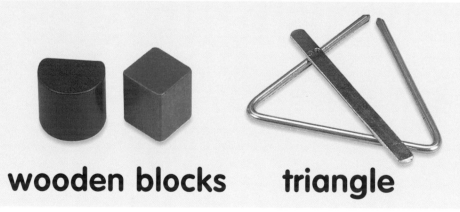

wooden blocks   **triangle**   **jug and cup of water**

▲ You could make sound effects for each picture, using the objects above.

story   sound effects

▼ Put the sounds together and tell the story in sound. Then you could record your sound story.

scrunchy paper

record

Further information for

Possible Activities

PAGES 4-5

Go on a sound walk around different parts of the school – both inside and outside. Ask children to keep quiet and to listen hard. Return to the classroom and talk about all the sounds they heard.

PAGES 6-7

Allow the children to try out many kinds of musical instruments. How do they play them? What kind of sound is made? Which ones do they like/dislike? How can they make the instrument sound soft? How can they make it sound loud?

Sort the instruments into groups, according to how they are played. Draw or write lists of the different groups.

Make some home-made musical instruments, using elastic bands over a beaker, sugar inside empty yoghurt pots or some empty cardboard tubes. How would the children play these?

PAGES 8-9

Ask children to predict the sounds they will hear in bed this evening, and make a list. The next day, ask them to remember what they actually heard. Compare the two different lists.

Find a big picture of a busy scene – e.g. a beach on a summer's day. Ask the children what sounds they would hear if they were there. Which ones would be loudest/softest?

PAGES 10-11

Ask the children to touch their throat as they speak or sing. Can they feel a difference when they make a high sound and when they make a low, growly sound?

Ask the children to find different animal sounds on a CD-ROM or other resource.

PAGES 12-13

Listen to a tape containing familiar sounds. Can the children identify them all?

Parents and Teachers

Ask the children to cover their ears and walk around a room. Is it easy to walk around if you cannot hear? Make sure the environment is safe and ask them to shut their eyes as well.

Hide different things (e.g. a marble, a cork, a pencil, a paper clip, rice, cotton wool) inside a box. Can children identify the object by shaking the box?

PAGES 14-15

Make a list or draw pictures of three sounds that can be heard from a long way away.

PAGES 16-17

Discuss how animals (e.g. rabbits) rely on their hearing to keep them safe. Some animals (e.g. birds, monkeys) call to one another when danger is close.

Make a list of all the vehicles that have sirens, bells, musical sounds or loudspeakers.

PAGES 18-19

Collect pictures that could be the starting point for literacy work about sounds (c.g. a rocket launching, a grasshopper, a waterfall). Make a list of sounds to suit each picture. Can the children guess the picture from the list of words?

PAGES 20-21

Ask the children to write a very simple story that could be told using sounds. Then ask them to collect objects that would make suitable sound effects. Record the sounds and perform the story.

Further Information

BOOKS FOR CHILDREN

The Best Ears in the World by Claire Llewellyn
(Hodder Wayland, 2002)

Hearing Sounds by Sally Hewitt
(Franklin Watts, 2000)

Listening and Hearing by Henry Pluckrose
(Franklin Watts, 2001)

Sound by Peter Riley
(Franklin Watts, 2001)

BOOKS FOR ADULTS

How to Sparkle at Science Investigations by Monica Huns
(Brilliant Publications)

WEBSITES

www.educate.org.uk

www.howstuffworks.com

www.learn.co.uk/glearning/primarylessons/ks1/sound2/default.asp

www.primaryresources.co.uk/science

Index